# THE FIRST CHRISTMAS

# THE FIRST CHRISTMAS
## Rachel Billington and Barbara Brown

COLLINS

William Collins Sons & Co Ltd
London · Glasgow · Sydney · Auckland
Toronto · Johannesburg

First published 1983
© Text Rachel Billington 1983
© Illustrations Barbara Brown 1983
ISBN 0 00 195048 7
Origination by Culver Graphics Litho Ltd
Printed in Italy
by Sagdos for Imago Publishing Ltd

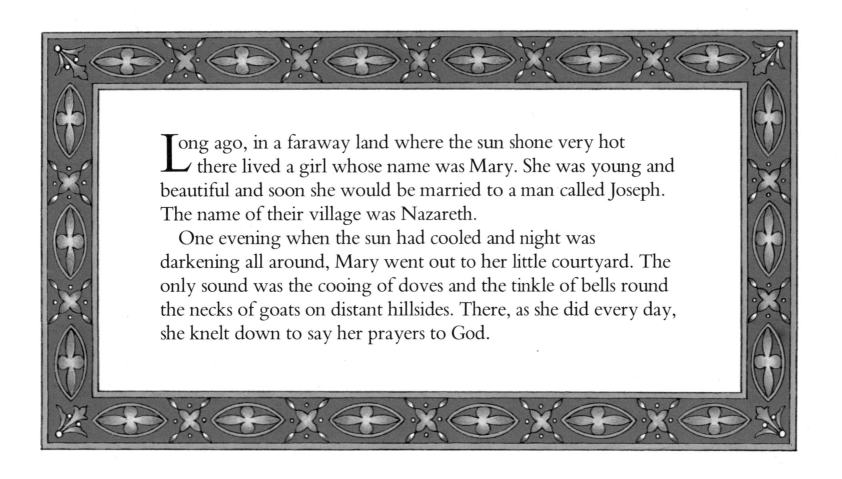

Long ago, in a faraway land where the sun shone very hot there lived a girl whose name was Mary. She was young and beautiful and soon she would be married to a man called Joseph. The name of their village was Nazareth.

One evening when the sun had cooled and night was darkening all around, Mary went out to her little courtyard. The only sound was the cooing of doves and the tinkle of bells round the necks of goats on distant hillsides. There, as she did every day, she knelt down to say her prayers to God.

But on this occasion her peace was broken. For suddenly she was surrounded by a light so brilliant that it was as if the sun had come up again. Out of the light a voice spoke like a trumpet:

"Hail Mary, full of grace, the Lord is with you!"

Poor Mary was nearly blinded and certainly very frightened, so she put her hands across her face. Then the voice spoke to her again, but in a calm, gentle way:

"Do not be afraid, Mary, for you have found favour with God."

Mary took her hands from her face. She realized that the light was from God and that the beautiful creature standing in front of her was an angel from heaven. No longer frightened, she listened very carefully.

"Behold, you will bear a son and you shall call him Jesus. He will be great and will be called the Son of the Most High and the Lord will make him King, as his ancestor, David, was King. And he will reign for ever and ever."

Then the angel was silent. Mary asked humbly: "But how can I have a baby when I'm not yet married?"

The angel answered:

"The Holy Spirit will guide you and the power of the Most High will be all around you. Therefore your child will be the Son of God. Your cousin Elizabeth is also going to have a baby, although everyone thought she was too old. For with God's help nothing is impossible!"

Mary bowed her head in obedience to God's wishes and said:

"I am the servant of the Lord. Let it happen just as you have said."

The angel left her then. And the brilliant light went too.

Once more Mary was alone in the dusky courtyard and it was almost as if she had been dreaming. But she knew it was all true. So she decided to visit her cousin Elizabeth as soon as possible.

Mary made preparations for her journey to Elizabeth, who lived up in the hills. She collected black olives and flat bread and white goat cheese. She packed them in saddle bags on either side of the donkey who would carry her through the narrow winding paths.

The next morning, when there was still a mist over the spring-green hills, she said goodbye to Joseph and her relations and set off. Even so, it was late when she arrived and she was very stiff and tired. But there was her cousin Elizabeth standing outside her house, the flowers like a carpet under her feet. As soon as Mary was near enough, she shouted out her name. At once Elizabeth saw her and, holding out her arms in welcome, called in a joyful voice:

"Blessed are you among women and blessed is the baby you are going to have."

And Mary was reminded of the angel's greeting. Elizabeth went on:
  "Why do I deserve a visit from the mother of my Lord? For when you called my name, my baby jumped with joy inside me. Blessed is she who believed in the message that came from heaven."
  Now Mary was even more certain that she would have a baby who was to be the Son of God. And there on the path before Elizabeth's house, with the donkey beside her, she sang out the most wonderful prayer:

My heart sings in praise of the Lord,
And my soul rejoices in God, my Saviour,
For he has remembered his humble maidservant.
Behold, from now on I will always be called blessed;
For almighty God has done great things for me.
His name is holy.
And he shows mercy to those who honour him
From generation to generation.
With his strong right hand
He has scattered the proud with their scheming hearts.
He has swept the high and mighty from their thrones
And raised up the poor and lowly;
He has filled the hungry with good things,
And the rich he has sent away empty-handed.
He has shown mercy to the people of Israel
As he promised to Abraham and his descendants
For ever and ever. Amen.

Afterwards Mary and Elizabeth kissed each other warmly and went together into the house. There Mary stayed for several months helping her cousin with her tasks, for the baby Elizabeth was carrying made her easily tired. And that baby was to be called John the Baptist, because when he grew up he would prepare people for baptism in the name of Jesus even before Jesus himself started his work.

But Mary went back home before John was born because she wanted to get ready for her own child's birth.

Now Joseph, the man Mary was
to marry, was a good man. He was
a carpenter, who worked hard all
day making chairs and tables and
sometimes more beautiful things,
carved with patterns of leaves and
flowers. When Mary told him she
was going to have a baby and the
baby was going to be the Lord, he
was naturally astonished. He even
wondered if he should marry her
now. But he thought and prayed
very hard. And one night an angel
appeared to him in his sleep and
told him that Mary's baby had
been sent to her by the Holy Spirit.
Now he believed Mary and
understood that he also had been
honoured. For it was his duty to
look after the mother of God and
after Jesus himself when he was
born.

So he and Mary were married
and lived together.

But looking after Mary turned out to be very difficult. For just before the baby was due, when Mary had prepared a cradle and all the things that were necessary, a ruling went out through the land where they lived. Every man must go and register his name and his wife's name at the town where his family first came from. This was because their land was ruled by a Roman emperor called Caesar Augustus who wanted to find out exactly how many people lived in the faraway corners of his empire. Joseph's family name was David and they had come from a small town called Bethlehem. Bethlehem was several days journey from Nazareth.

So Mary had to leave her comfortable home and mount the donkey again. But this time it was winter and at night it grew very dark and cold. And in the day it sometimes rained and when they crossed high ground it snowed, which would have been exhausting even if she hadn't been expecting a baby. Joseph walked beside her leading the donkey, and at night, if they could find nowhere to stay, he wrapped her in his warm coat made of sheep's wool. Mary never complained. She thought of her very special baby and was happy.

After several days, they began to meet other travellers, some going one way, some another because everyone had to find his family town. They exchanged news and Joseph heard that Bethlehem was already filled with people waiting to register their names. He was worried because he knew the town was not very big and he must find somewhere comfortable for Mary. But he could not hurry the little donkey with its precious load.

At last they saw Bethlehem high up on the hillside in front of them. Smoke from hundreds of fires rose from it, for it was already evening and the air was cold as ice.

By the time they entered the city, it was nearly dark. The narrow streets, the fires from the houses and the lighted windows made the air seem warmer. But Joseph knew he must find somewhere to stay as soon as possible. This was not easy. Everywhere he looked there were people: old, young; men, women; children and babies. The strong and healthy seemed to be enjoying such a large gathering as if it were a party. Some of them were selling bread. Others sold sugary sweets, woven rugs, candles, oil for lamps or even lambs or kid goats. Some were too old or sick or cross at their sudden upheaval to do more than wail their misery or wag their long grey beards. And everywhere the children ran, shouting and laughing and tripping up anyone who got in their way.

Joseph stopped one young boy and asked him if he knew a good clean place for them to stay. The boy laughed in his face and ran off shouting, "Everywhere's full since midday. You'd be lucky to find a hole for a bed!" Joseph carried on asking at every house or inn, for Mary had told him that she would be having the baby that very night.

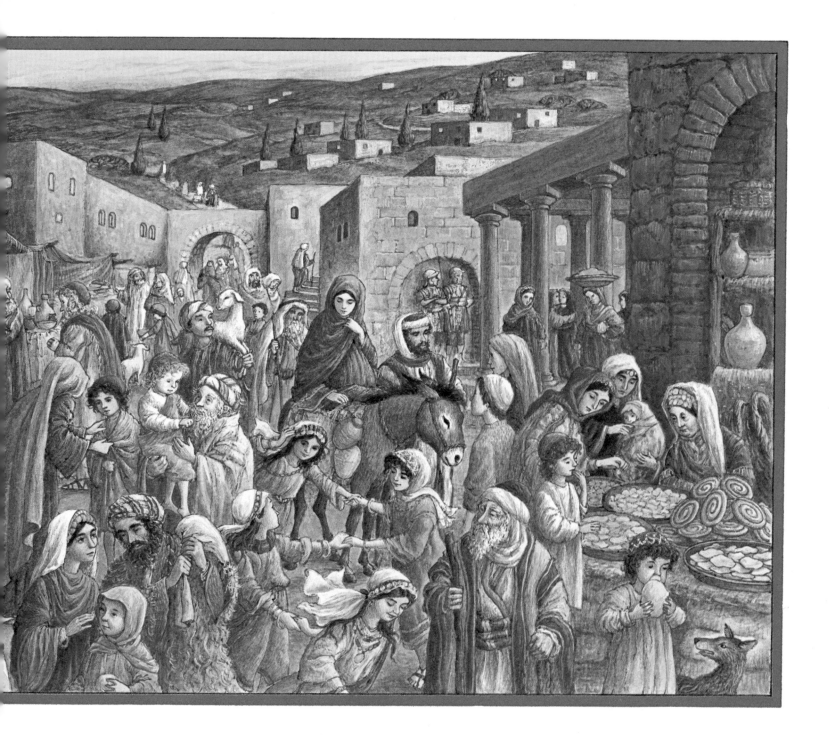

After nearly two hours walking through the rough streets, when it looked as though the donkey would collapse if he went another step, Joseph approached a small inn on the edge of town. It was his very last hope, for beyond it lay only the cold hillside from which they had come. His hopes were not high because he could see through the lighted windows the outlines of many people.

Nevertheless he knocked on the heavy door. It was opened quickly by a burly man who immediately bawled out: "No room! No room!" Then he stopped. Although he was big and noisy, he had a kind face and he had just seen poor Mary slip off the donkey's back. She stood trembling with cold and the fear that she would find no place to shelter her baby's head.

"Well, well." The innkeeper

took a step out from his doorway. He pointed round the corner of the building. "There's a stable more or less empty. Save for the ox and ass, that is. But they're friendly enough and will keep you warm."

The innkeeper watched them go, shaking his head. It was a strange place for a young girl to have a baby. Just then he was called from inside and he shut the door consoling himself with the thought of the clean straw he'd put down that morning.

To Mary and Joseph the stable was a welcome and beautiful place. The ox and the ass, large gentle creatures, were eating hay from a manger. Mary began to get everything ready for the birth. She realized that the manger would make a good crib and covered the hay with a soft cloth. She laid out swaddling clothes, a white square with a long strip at one corner in which new babies were wrapped. When she had finished her preparations she waited peacefully.

Later that night, on the dark hills beyond the town, there showed a flickering orange light. It came from a fire which some shepherds had lit. They camped out every night watching to see that their flocks of sheep didn't stray.

Suddenly the whole sky was filled with a dazzling light and there appeared an angel of the Lord just as had appeared to Mary. And they too were frightened and hid their faces. The dogs dozing beside them trembled and the sheep huddled together as if there were a storm approaching.

But the angel spoke gently: "Do not be afraid. For behold, I bring you good news of great joy which will come to all the people."

So the shepherds uncovered their eyes.

The angel went on: "Today a Saviour is born for you in the city of David. And that Saviour is Christ the Lord. You will know it is he because you will find a baby wrapped in swaddling clothes, lying in a manger."

All at once this angel was joined by a whole chorus of other angels, singing God's praises:

*"Glory to God in the highest,*
*And peace to his people on earth."*

They finished their song and suddenly it was dark again. Even the fire had gone out. The shepherds felt cold and stiff as if a long time had passed since they had been quietly lying on the hillside. They stood up and stamped their feet and hardly dared look at each other for their excitement. At last an old man spoke up: "Let us go to Bethlehem and see this baby." So they put their dogs on guard round the sheep, and hurried to the town.

I t was nearly dawn by the time the shepherds reached Bethlehem. The frost made the ground hard underfoot and their breath blew white in the cold air. Only a few early risers, bakers and herdsmen, were stirring from their sleep. The streets were so quiet and empty it hardly seemed the same town as the evening before.

But in one place a lamp glowed as it had all night. And two people who had been awake all night sat watching by a manger. The two people were Mary and Joseph and in that manger lay the baby Jesus. He was only a few hours old.

Soon the shepherds knocked their crooks against the old wooden door, not sure yet if they had found the right stable. Joseph opened it and put his finger to his lips. The baby slept. The shepherds came in and fell to their knees; they knew they were in the presence of God. The baby opened his eyes as if he knew who they were and why they'd come.

They explained how the angel had appeared to them and told them where to find the little baby who was to be Saviour of all the world. They gave him a lamb they'd brought as a present. And they gave sheep's milk and sheep's wool to Mary and Joseph. They wished that they could give more valuable presents. But Joseph made them understand that they had been chosen as the first people to see Jesus because they were poor.

So the shepherds went out into the town filled with joy. The streets were busy now and they told everyone they met what they had seen. Later they returned to their sheep, still guarded by their faithful dogs.

Meanwhile, inside the stable, Mary thought over what the shepherds had told her. She looked at her little baby. It was very difficult to understand that he would grow up to save the world. But she knew that was what God had planned for him. She must do whatever was wanted of her.

So far, as you can see, the story of Jesus' birth is a very humble one. Mary and Joseph were simple people who worked with their hands.

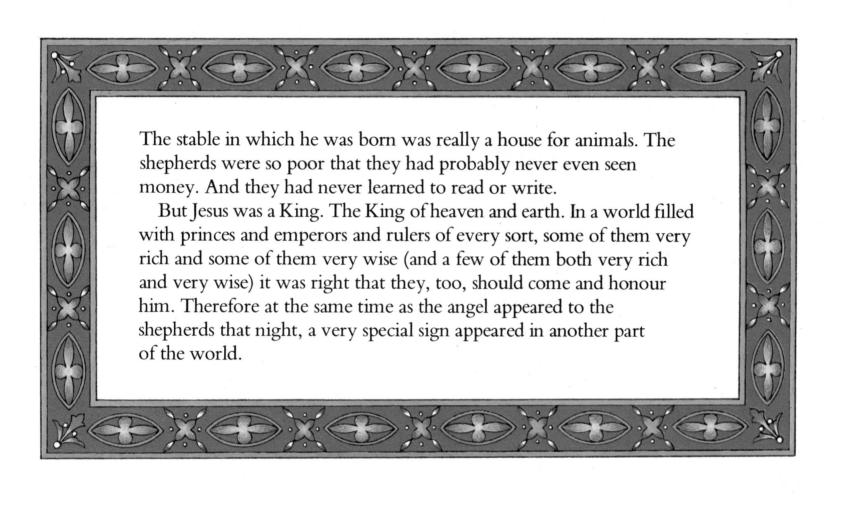

The stable in which he was born was really a house for animals. The shepherds were so poor that they had probably never even seen money. And they had never learned to read or write.

But Jesus was a King. The King of heaven and earth. In a world filled with princes and emperors and rulers of every sort, some of them very rich and some of them very wise (and a few of them both very rich and very wise) it was right that they, too, should come and honour him. Therefore at the same time as the angel appeared to the shepherds that night, a very special sign appeared in another part of the world.

A star rose in the East. It rose so suddenly and shone so brilliantly that it could only mean the birth of a new king. Three rich and clever kings, who lived in three different countries, saw the star. They all knew well the meaning of the skies. One, who was called Caspar, found its position on a map. The second, Melchior, watched it from the top of a tall tower. And the third, Balthasar, saw its reflection in a pool of clear water. They all saw it begin to move. At once each one made preparations for a long journey, for they knew that if they followed the star it would lead them to the place where this new king was born.

As they were so important they travelled with many attendants and slaves. They carried with them three very special presents. One brought gold, which is the right kind of present for a king. Another brought frankincense which is used in churches to make the air smell sweet. That honoured the baby as God as well as man. And the third brought myrrh, which is used in funerals. For these wise men knew that later Jesus must sacrifice his life for the world.

The rich and clever kings did not travel on little old donkeys. They had swift camels with haughty faces and very long legs. But they had a great way to come and it was forty days before the star finally stopped over Bethlehem.

By then Mary and Jesus had moved out of the stable and into a room. Jesus was no longer in swaddling clothes, and he could sit up on his mother's lap.

Already the news of his birth had travelled far and wide and there had

been many visitors. Even so, no one had ever seen such a splendid sight as the arrival of the three kings. Everybody crowded after them into the little room, admiring their gorgeous clothes and crowds of servants.

But the moment the new visitors saw the baby in Mary's arms, they fell down on their knees and bent their heads onto the floor. In front of Jesus, they were as humble as the humblest shepherd. Those who watched saw this and realized that truly a great King and a Saviour had been born among them.

So ends the story of the first Christmas. Jesus was born. God was made man and lived among us.

It is only the beginning of the story of Jesus. For that little baby who was held so tenderly in his mother's arms came into the world to help all of us.

By his teaching and by the way he lived he showed us how we should lead our lives on earth. By his suffering and death on the cross he made it possible for us to join him in heaven.

All this began when the angel came to Mary long ago.